Magnets & Batteries

▲ David Evans and Claudette Williams □

DORLING KINDERSLEY
LONDON • NEW YORK • STUTTGART

A DORLING KINDERSLEY BOOK

Project Editor Stella Love
Art Editor Sara Nunan
Designer Cheryl Telfer
Managing Editor Jane Yorke
Managing Art Editor Chris Scollen
Production Jayne Wood
Photography by Susanna Price
U.S. Assistant Editor Lara Tankel

First American Edition, 1993
2 4 6 8 10 9 7 5 3 1

Published in the United States by
Dorling Kindersley, Inc., 232 Madison Avenue
New York, New York 10016

Cataloguing-in-Publication data for this book
is available from the Library of Congress

ISBN 1-56458-346-5

Reproduced by J. Film Process Singapore Pte., Ltd.
Printed and bound in Belgium by Proost

Dorling Kindersley would like to thank the following for their help
in producing this book: Coral Mula (for safety symbol artwork);
Mark Richards (for jacket design); Berol Limited, King's Lynn;
and the Franklin Delano Roosevelt School, London.
Dorling Kindersley would also like to give special thanks to the following for
appearing in this book: Natalie Agada; Gregory Coleman; Sophia El Kaddar;
Caroline Graham; Tony Locke; Gemma Loke; Paul Miller; Tanya Pham;
Maxwell Ralph; Elizabeth Robert; Nicholas Smith; and Simon Spencer.

Contents

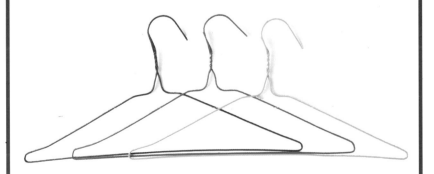

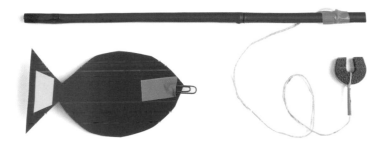

Note to parents and teachers

Young children are forever asking questions about the things they see, touch, hear, smell, and taste. The **Let's Explore Science** series aims to foster children's natural curiosity and encourages them to use their senses to find out about science. Each book features a variety of experiments based on one topic, which draw on a young child's everyday experiences. By investigating familiar activities, such as bouncing a ball, making cookies, or clapping hands, young children will learn that science plays an important part in the world around them.

Investigative approach

Young children can only begin to understand science if they are stimulated to think and find out for themselves. For these reasons, an open-ended questioning approach is used in the **Let's Explore Science** books and, wherever possible, results of experiments are not shown. Children are encouraged to make their own scientific discoveries, and to interpret them according to their own ideas. This investigative approach to learning makes science exciting and not just about acquiring "facts." This way of learning will assist children in many areas of their education.

Using the books

Before starting an experiment, check the text and pictures to ensure that you have gathered any necessary equipment. Allow children to help in this process and to suggest alternative materials to use. Once ready, it is important to let children decide how to carry out the experiment and what the result means to them. You can help by asking questions, such as, "What do you think will happen?" or "What did you do?"

Equipment

All the experiments can be carried out easily at home with inexpensive materials. Many toy stores stock magnets and the necessary electrical components should be readily available from general electrical or hardware stores.

It does not matter if the components are not identical to those shown in the book.

Guide to experiments

The *Guide to experiments* on pages 28-29 is intended to help parents, teachers, or helpers using this book with children. It gives an outline of the scientific principles underlying the experiments, includes useful tips for carrying out the activities, suggests alternative equipment to use, and additional activities to try.

Safe experimenting

This symbol appears next to experiments where children may require adult supervision or assistance, such as, when they are heating things or using sharp tools.

About this book

In **Magnets and Batteries**, young children are challenged to find out about static electricity, magnetism, and current electricity as they create static charges, use magnets, and build simple circuits.

By trying these activities, children will discover that:

- friction on some objects can create an electrostatic charge that may attract or repel other charged objects;

- magnets have north and south poles that attract opposite poles and repel like poles;

- magnets will only attract or repel objects made of some metals;

- a magnet can be used to magnetize another object provided that the object is made of a ferrous metal;

- a simple circuit can be made with a battery and wires that will make a light bulb, buzzer, or motor work;

- some materials will conduct electricity while others, such as insulators, do not.

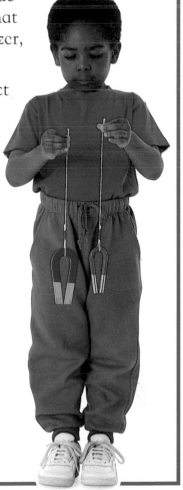

With your help, young children will enjoy exploring the world of science and discover that finding out is fun.

David Evans and Claudette Williams

What happens if you rub it?

What happens when you rub balloons or plastic things and hold them near other things?

Balloons
Rub a balloon against your clothes and ask a friend to do the same.

What happens when you hang the two balloons next to each other?

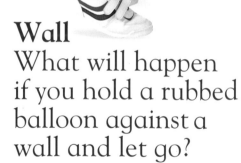

Wall
What will happen if you hold a rubbed balloon against a wall and let go?

Plastic ruler
What happens if you rub a plastic ruler with a plastic bag and hold the ruler over small pieces of paper? Now try rubbing the ruler with silk or cotton material.

Plastic straws
Rub some straws with a plastic bag and put them side by side on a table. What happens?

Salt and pepper
Can you pick up grains of salt and pepper with a rubbed balloon?

Hair
What happens when you rub a balloon and hold it close to someone's hair?

11

What does a magnet do?

What can you find
out about magnets?

Finding magnets
Can you find any
magnets like these?

Feeling magnets
What do you feel when
you hold two magnets end
to end? What happens if
you turn one around?

**Hanging
magnets**
What will
happen
when you
hang two
magnets
side by side
on strings?

**Piling
magnets**
Can you
make a
pile of
magnets?

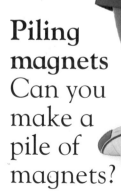

12

Using magnets
Gather some
small objects.

What happens when you
hold a magnet near to them?

Testing magnets
What happens when you hold
your magnet near other
objects in the room?

Which things
will not stick
to a magnet?

13

Can you make a magnet?

Can you use one magnet to
make another magnet?

Metal fork
Do metal
things stick
to a fork?

Hold a magnet on one end of the fork.
Do metal things stick to the fork now?

What happens if you
take the magnet away?

Metal spoon
Can you make a spoon into a magnet? Rub the spoon with one end of a magnet for a long time.

Coat hanger
Can you turn a wire coat hanger into a magnet?

How will you know if the spoon is now a magnet?

Tap the spoon on the ground. Is the spoon still a magnet?

How strong is a magnet?

Test your magnet to find out how strong it is.

Water
Will your magnet work through water? Can you get paper clips out of a plastic bottle of water without getting your fingers wet?

Big objects
What is the biggest object you can pick up with your magnet?

Now try with two magnets. Can you pick up bigger things?

Are some magnets stronger than others?

Cloth
Will a magnet work if you wrap it in cloth, paper, or aluminum foil? Will it work through wood?

Paper clips
How many paper clips can you pick up with a magnet?

Small objects
Fix a magnet to the floor with tape. How close to the magnet can you push small metal objects before they are pulled toward it?

Can you use a magnet?

Make some magnet games. How can you use a magnet to make a compass?

Fishing game
Cut out lots of paper fish and fix a paper clip on each one.

Make a fishing rod with some string, a magnet, and a stick.

Treasure hunt
Ask a friend to hide some magnets and metal objects in sand. How can you find all the things?

How many fish can you catch in one try?

Using a compass

Hang a magnet on a piece of string. Then use a compass to find out which way the magnet points.

Do all magnets point the same way?

Making a compass

 Make a large sewing needle into a magnet by rubbing it with a magnet.

Now float a small plastic lid in a bowl of water and put the needle on it.

Can you tell which way is north?

What does a battery do?

Try these experiments to find out about batteries.

 Never try to cut open a battery.

Looking at batteries
Do you have any batteries like the ones shown here? How many different shapes and sizes can you find?

Look closely at the batteries you have. In what ways are they all the same?

Using batteries
Can you make things work by putting batteries into them? How many batteries do things need? Where do you put the batteries?

What will happen if you put the batteries in the other way around?

How do you know when something needs new batteries?

21

Can you make a circuit?

What things do you need to make a small light bulb light up?

light bulbs

Handle light bulbs with care.

Finding things
Do you have any of these things?

crocodile clip

bulb holder

wire

Making a circuit
Join together some wires, a battery, and a light bulb in a holder. Where do the ends of the wires go?

Will the light bulb light up?

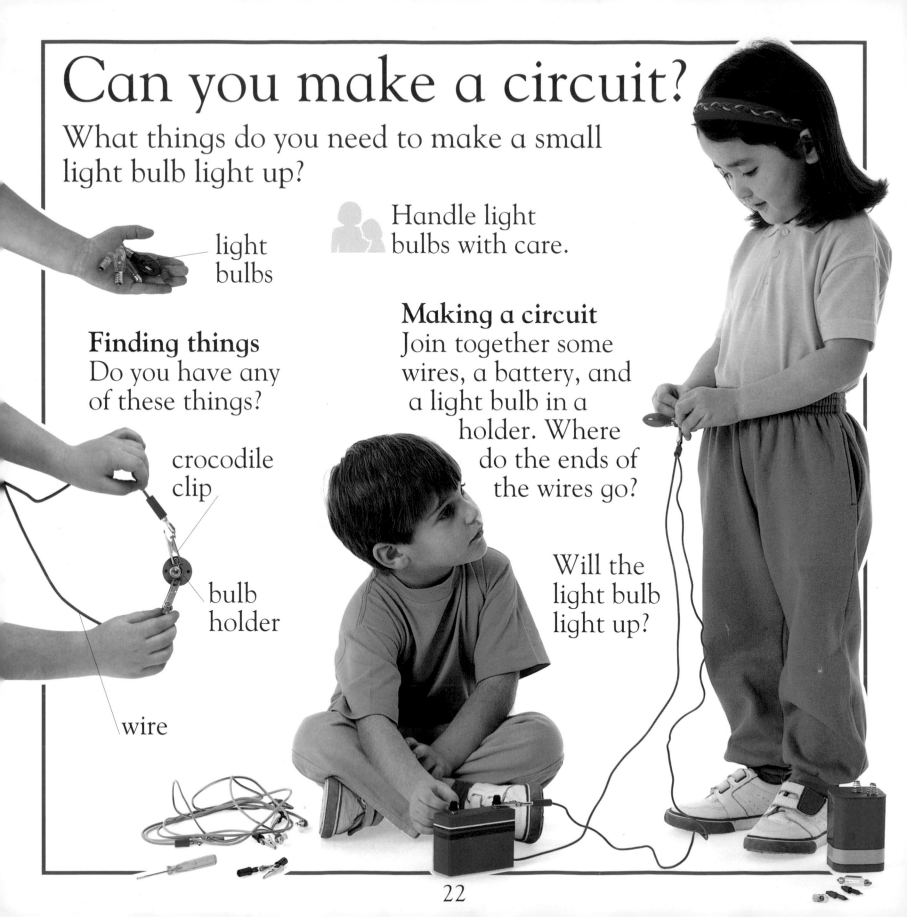

Testing for conductors

Will the light bulb work if you add a plastic ruler into the circuit? What happens if you use a metal fork instead of the ruler?

What do you think will happen if you try each of the things on the table?

Can you use string instead of wires to make a circuit?

Can you make a big circuit?

Try these experiments to make circuits with lights, buzzers, a switch, and a fan that spins around.

switch

buzzer

Two light bulbs
How can you make two light bulbs light up at the same time? Can you add a buzzer to your circuit and a switch to turn it on and off?

How does a switch work?

24

motor

spindle

stiff paper

Motor and fan

Draw a fan shape on some paper and cut it out. Push the fan onto the motor spindle. Can you make the motor turn the fan?

Buzzer and bulb

Can you make a buzzer and a light bulb work at the same time?

Fan or bulb

Can you build a big circuit to make a fan spin around or a light bulb work separately?

What can electricity do?

How many things do you see that plug into a socket to make them work? What do you know about the electricity that makes them work?

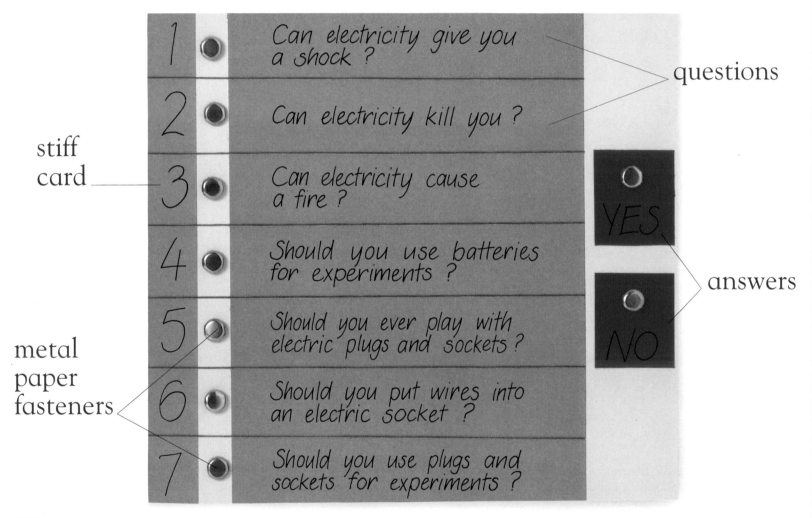

1. Can electricity give you a shock?
2. Can electricity kill you?
3. Can electricity cause a fire?
4. Should you use batteries for experiments?
5. Should you ever play with electric plugs and sockets?
6. Should you put wires into an electric socket?
7. Should you use plugs and sockets for experiments?

questions

stiff card

metal paper fasteners

YES

NO

answers

Electricity quiz game

Can you find out the correct answers to these questions? Ask an adult to help you make a quiz game like this one. You will need card, nine paper fasteners, aluminum foil, and tape.

card

paper
fasteners

tape

aluminum foil

Making the quiz board
Place two pieces of foil on the back of the quiz board. Push the nine paper fasteners through the card and foil, exactly as shown.

Open out the paper fasteners and cover them with tape.

Playing the quiz game
Make a circuit like this to play the game. Place the end of one wire on the paper fastener next to a question.

Place the other wire on the fastener next to your answer.

Can you guess the correct answer?

If you are right, the bulb will light up.

27

Index

Guide to experiments

The notes below briefly outline the scientific principles underlying the experiments and include suggestions for alternative equipment to use and activities to try.

What happens if you rub it? 10-11

By experimenting with friction to give balloons and plastic materials an electrostatic charge, children will become aware of the forces of repulsion between like charges, and attraction between unlike charges.

What does a magnet do? 12-13

A magnet has two poles called north and south respectively. Children will feel the forces involved when the north poles (like poles) of two magnets repel each other and the north pole of one magnet attracts the south pole (unlike poles) of another magnet. The experiments show that magnets only attract objects containing ferromagnetic metals, such as iron or steel.

Can you make a magnet? 14-15

Permanent magnets remain magnetic all the time. This magnetism may be induced in metals such as iron and steel when a permanent magnet is held close to them. If iron or steel objects are rubbed or stroked with a permanent magnet, they may become permanent magnets, too. If magnets are dropped or knocked, their magnetism may be lost.

How strong is a magnet? 16-17

The experiments lead children to realize that different magnets are of different strengths and will attract some metal objects from various distances. Their force can be strong enough to affect heavy objects and to work through thick materials.

Can you use a magnet? 18-19

In these activities children use their knowledge of magnets to make and play games. When a magnet is suspended, it will always come to rest pointing to magnetic north. This is because the Earth itself is a huge magnet and its north pole attracts another magnet's south pole. Children use this principle to make their own compass.

What does a battery do? 20-21

Common batteries are safe to use for experiments but 9-volt, nickel cadmium, and rechargeable batteries should be avoided. Children should not open up batteries to look inside. The activities will help children realize that there is a wide range of batteries and that to operate devices, the batteries must be inserted in a particular way.

Can you make a circuit? 22-23

Children will learn that an electric charge flows through wires connected to a battery if a circuit is made, and this charge can light up a small bulb. Batteries of 6 volts or less should be used, and the bulbs should have a voltage rating to match. A wire placed across the battery terminals may cause a short circuit. Ensure that a light bulb, or other device, is built into the circuit to avoid this.

Can you make a big circuit? 24-25

Children are challenged to make switches, buzzers, and motors work, and to operate two or more devices at the same time. Children will build either a series circuit, i.e., one circuit with each component inserted in a line, or parallel circuits, i.e., each component is built into a separate circuit but powered by the same battery.

What can electricity do? 26-27

The quiz game will make children aware of the dangers of misusing electricity and will raise safety points for further discussion about plugs and sockets. The foil pieces on the back of the board must be separate and not touch each other if the game is to work properly.

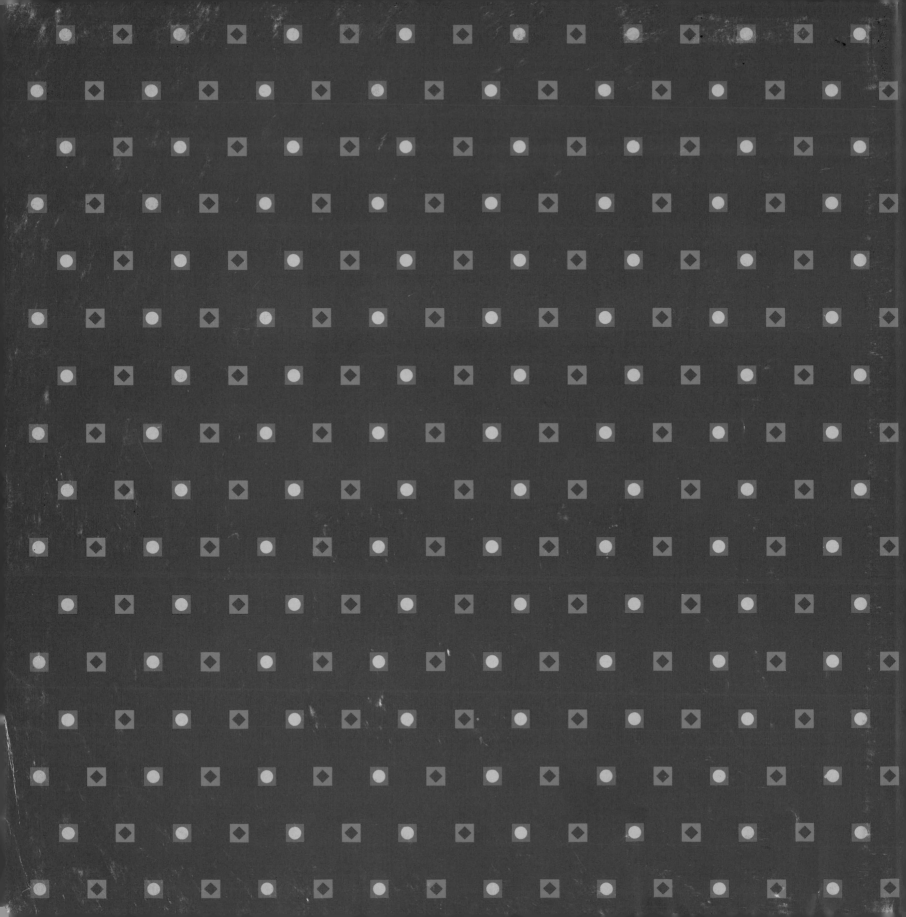